The Knowledge of the Past and the Future

The Knowledge of the Past and the Future

A Logical Knowledge Series
about Human Existence, Leading
to the Attainment of a Good Success

BARISUA SIMEON

PARTRIDGE
A Penguin Random House Company

To order additional copies of this book, contact
Partridge India
000 800 10062 62
orders.india@partridgepublishing.com

www.partridgepublishing.com/india

Contents

Dedicated

To God Almighty, the Creator of the heavens and the earth, at Whose expense came about the existence of humans, the unique, precious family of Simeon Nwamae, and all my distinguished honourable readers and fellow existences.

Introduction

No wrongly analyzed human existence can ever lead to the attainment of a good success. Rather, it should be based as much on a logical existentialist thinking manner as life requires.

This series is about *human existence*: the *indefeasible logo* of the living, the success-oriented, and the future-inclined. Why? No existence, no occurrences of human deeds; whereas every achievement is as a result of human deeds. This is the reason why every earthly existence ought to carry out right the analysis of the effectiveness of his or her earthly stay. How do you do that? It's simply by logically tracing your life source; studying your existence so far. Naturally, nowadays generally carried out is this conclusion that is based on the belief that as much worthless as any obvious inexistence are the unsuccessful people – the less privileged or probably the slapped (or deserted) by nature. This is caused by nothing else than just failing to trace one's life source in a proper logical fashion. And every good success is embodied in the right life source of every earthly existence.

In a nutshell, a great many individuals struggle because they have unconsciously chosen to. Many are poor because of their logicality thinking inability about human existence, in general. Many are successfully unstable because of their inability to maintain their logicality analytical ability about human existence. Again worth addressing is but of those who have unconsciously desired not to activate this human-existence logicality thinking ability at all. This is one of the reasons why many a person has failed, on earth, whereas success is not an exclusive of any human being. Why, then, do many struggle? This now makes us to realize the obvious purpose for the writing of this book, clearly designed to help remind us the reason why we ought to reflect on and analyze our general human existence, our various pasts, our maybe present, and our distinct futures. And so this book is but designed to help us make no longer redundant our human logicality thinking ability about our existence. Without this ability, which is the key to any particular success, one is liable to keep knocking, begging, and crying at the door for a good success to come out, whereas it is what is achievable only by simply unlocking it with the *key*. In other words, every good and special success must be unlocked, just like any good and special commodity is bound to be pretty costlier than others. You see? This is the reason why we really have to know our pasts. It is as naturally highly penal as what usually befalls whoever fails to learn from histories. Many are only skillfully but not practically successful. This implies that they are truly skillful enough to earn them a good success but unfortunately do not have the key to unlock for their skills a manifestation arena. This key is therefore very important. How do you produce your key, anyway? It is as easy as simply identifying your manifestation area in life. You, therefore, ought to study your past, your maybe present, and then relate it to your future. In other words, you've got to know your past from your maybe present, study them as much logically as you can, to know which exactly is your future. You know why? A great many individuals do not know what usually brings about their past, their maybe present, and their future. This is because what you might see as your present is actually the future of your past, which soon/eventually becomes another past to your next future. When, then, do we really have a present? That is the question. And so until you know this, your conception about life will hardly produce for you any good success. Additionally, you may be but obviously not succeeding well. This implies that your success is not a good one. The Bible also reveals this, saying: *The blessing* of the Lord makes one rich, and He adds no sorrow with it (Proverbs 10:22). Thus, suffering is not an affiliate of a good success.

It is this no-present knowledge analysis, therefore, that can create the consciousness or realization that if one must succeed, one must not relax; because, there is actually no room for relaxation. Otherwise, your existence will confuse and disillusion you. It is this simple understanding that can produce your success key. Logically, therefore, if one must make out something of life, one must not have to imbibe this present-living mentality. Rather, you have to see that *apparent present* as your *current future*; which implies that if it is somewhat awkward or unproductive, you're going to need to work harder enough to attain a better one. Believe you me: what robs a great many individuals of their successes, daily, is the lack of this simple understanding. It is because *consciousness* is the only *instrument* for the creation of one's desire for the attainment of a good success. In other words, every success requires extraordinary awareness for the desire for it. And so if you sensitively see your today (present) as rather your current future, which soon becomes your past, working out your next future, and never your present, you will certainly always be desirous of a greater success. In addition, therefore, to help enhance our understanding is this assertion that every living being has but only one present in his lifetime, but that which is greatly pervaded by some indefeasibly generic childhood reasoning. This means that the very day a child is born is the only day that could be considered as a present, since it is not preceded by any other. And so the two inevitable periods that are inextricably tied to our from-time-to-time living are the past and the future. This is a natural phenomenon that once one fails to think, desire and act based on it, one becomes an automatic failure, whereas, perhaps, no rational human being would delight in becoming a failure in life. And for the fact that failure is but tied only to wrong reasoning, it becomes absolutely inevitable when you patronize it with your insensitivity-based kind of reasoning. Thus, every good success requires a pretty degree of proper logical reasoning, which implies that your human sensitivity and psychological abilities must always be active. However, a great many people usually complain as to their inability to think accurately logically, implying that a disciplinary measure is never a bi-product of their thinking act. *Discipline* is another essential device for the founding of your success *edifice*. So if one must attain a good success, the desire for it must be based on what is here termed as *sensitivity-disciplinary-psychological* act. With this tripartite principle, here comes your good success already!

Additionally, the only guarantee for your good success is but by first knowing who you are, where you are, what exactly you want, and where you are going. Without this simple knowledge or realization, one will always be a candidate of failure. You see? This now makes it indisputably essential to have to study your past and relate it to your current future. In other words, everyone has to study their various pasts and relate them to their distinctive personalities, with a view to knowing who they are and what they've been capable of (doing) over the years, in order to know how to make accurate adjustments. This implies that why a great many people fail (in life) is because of making inaccurate adjustments, resulting to their not exactly knowing their real capabilities. John V. Lombardi reveals similarly, saying: *The past fascinates us.... We expect that the examples of past behaviours can teach us the right and just and proper way.* He also adds that *history never stays in the past but engages us at every twist and turn in our contemporary search for the future.* Invariably, therefore, if one cannot study and learn from one's past, one, likewise, cannot study and learn from another's past behaviour or history. However, as we move properly into the main journey of the reading of this book, the essence of studying our past will not only be glaringly inevitable, but also compulsorily ideal. Your past is your success reservoir!

Chapter One

The Knowledge of the
Past and the Future

*Understand your past, your current future
(commonly known as present), to better aim
at a greater future.*

Very clearly and/or naturally common is the fact that everyone has a past, but certainly distinct from that of the next fellow. Why? It's because human behaviours differ, which boils down to our having to convey information differently and bringing about diverse thoughts and experiences. This is the reason why humans are bound to react to situations differently. Thus, the way you understand a thing is the same way you approach it; meanwhile every situation or experience has a peculiar story to yield. Therefore, your individual experience creates for you a unique story. In other words, everyone has a special story to tell. And as such, your experience is the *tool* for the creation of your own past, making yours indisputably different from others'. Therefore your own past is in no way relevant to the existence of another person, but it can be learnt from, only if it is ethical or rational enough. None other than yourself can doctor the effectiveness of your own past, except you just feel like to have them help you analyze it. However, such an analysis is highly prone to fail in its course, because of not being purposed on something effectible. Why? It is because no matter what one says about the destiny of the other, no alteration can occur, unless you decide to be myopic and then begin to act based on their misconception about your own destiny or existence. *Destiny* is a decision-based *thing*. Many are so inquisitive as to may want to know why the talk about *destiny* in relation to the word *past*. Yes. Your destiny is the *child* of your past. How do I mean? It's what is usually known as *future*, given birth to by your past. You see? So once you allow your past to be awkward, your destiny – your future – will equally be awkward.

Therefore if you *kill* your past – by your illegal deeds, you've automatically put an end to your destiny – your future. In other words, logically speaking, your past is the *forerunner* of your existence. But the question is, *what is your past?* This question is but really one among few which are bound to evolve countless answers from a great many because of their fascinating ideal effects. If, thus, we want to better off the understanding of our discourse, knowing this becomes a priority. As we earlier disclosed that everyone has their various ways of conveying information, your experience from it is what brings about your own past. And as such, your daily experiences are what bring about your past, revealing that your past is embodied in what you do on a daily basis. Logically speaking, therefore, the past is as equally embodied in one's future as the future in the past. If you find it somewhat confusing, try to imagine why humans are always considerably dependent on the experiences of the days before, relating them to that of the current, in order to have a clear-cut view on the current one. In other words, both past and current experiences are *symbiotic* in nature. This is exactly what happens between your past and your future. However, to broach the main deliberation, it is germane to know that there are but only two pervading periods in the existence of *man* – the past and the future. Why no present? We find out soon.

What we really have to bear in mind is that in no way is this a deliberation in isolation, but how to make this knowledge an instrument for the actualization of a good success. But having said all that, believing that you already understand the difference between the past and the future, how, then, can one make this knowledge an instrument enough to produce a good success? First, believe in your past. Second, believe that you rather have a current future and not necessarily a present. Third, understand the interdependency between your past and your future. Fourth, don't feel satisfied with your current-future success level; aim at something greater and believe you can achieve it. Above all, always believe you can make a change. With all this, your greater success is sure! To back it up with Napoleon's *what-your-mind-can-conceive-and-believe-your-mind-can-achieve-it* ideal, success is individually determined. No mortal being can alter your own decision, except God, or you just desire to be myopic in life. This is also the reason why no one can automatically better off another's situation, most likely a poor person's. However, one can only help the other to create the reawakening for the desire of a good/greater success, but certainly not to do the decision-making for him or her. And so the only *carnivore* that is capable of *robbing* one's ability to decide for oneself is this ignorance of the knowledge of one's past. What we are here saying is like the case of to have to study the origin or history of something, to improve its function. In like manner, studying your past is but the only instrument that can bring about a rapid change to your existence. Take this example: if you must achieve the tubers yielded by your sown cassava stems, you must trace their roots; without which you cannot locate them. Therefore the benefit of everything is naturally tied to their roots. And so, as a human being, what do you think is your *root*? In this case, it is your past. If, however, you are so discerning as to the fact that most trees' fruits are usually achieved without to have to trace their roots, would you therefore cut off their roots and still expect any more yields? This is clearly the major reason why a great many persons now struggle; whereas they are yet toiling, their roots are already excavated, rendering them orphans amidst divine affluence. Additionally, once you are yet to know what we are here saying is like, you certainly find it rather difficult to know what exactly to do and better off your situation. Therefore if you must do things right, by knowing what exactly to do before or after the other, you must reflect on certain things. Once you reflect on things past, there will be this logicality thinking ability for you to begin to attend to things rationally. If you must study your past appropriately, therefore, you must learn to think logically enough; that which has made a great many to fail woefully, nowadays. Take for example, if you must think accurately, you must try and reflect on and redirect past occurrences to current happenings. It is like how natural it is for a nation, for instance, to toil under the filthy hands of a series of mistakes, once she fails to learn from histories. Look, your past is your *key*! How? This is because it is the determining factor for the attainment of your future expectation. For instance, the kind of foundation being laid by a child's parents usually manifests in time to come. If the foundation is negative or positive, it certainly speaks either way. And so one who says, for instance*: this child was not given a good foundation by his or her parents*, is not mistaken at all. And the only remedy to such a horrible situation is but to start again from the scratch, beginning to try as much to restructure the foundation as you can; otherwise, such a child will continually be considered as immoral and then deserted by all. Similarly, therefore, if your past requires restructuring and you're rather hobbling along with it, the wrongness of it will but be repellent to your expectations, resulting to dryness and/or unsuccessfulness. Wow! You know what? Life is a give-and-take lottery. Once you give out wrongly, you certainly receive wrongly, all determined by time. Ok, why is it biblical as to one to have to carry out absolute restitution for one's immoral or ungodly acts? That is the question! Why? It's because while doing that, you're invariably recycling the wrongness of your morality foundation. The word *foundation* is a divine but delicate thing. This is the reason why every logical and rational existence ought to have been thinking but analytically, saying: how is my current success level like? How was it like yesterday? How started it I? Am I really improving, or I should adopt another strategy? In this way, your past would certainly be useful and helpful to you. However, we seem not to be improving greatly because we've failed to utilize the effectiveness of our pasts. For instance, if you don't keep abreast with the exact colour of paint you applied previously on your house wall in your memory, and you'd love to improve on its beautification later, you will pretty fail in such course. Similarly, when trying to change to another church attire, for instance, it is ideal that you try and reflect on the very one worn previously. Or is there anyone who can comfortably put on a particular attire to church every day, if something is not amiss financially? I doubt. You know why? It's simply because everyone desires positive changes. Therefore if you don't desire positive changes, you fail to reflect. On the contrary, what makes entrepreneurs unusually successful is simply because they reflect so greatly on their little beginnings and try as much to make them useful and empowering to their current levels as they can.

Therefore if you throw away your past, you've indirectly demolished the foundation of your current level, keeping it at the risk of collapsing at any time. You see? No right-thinking, successful man can toil with his foundation, let alone allowing anyone else to. And that's why it is impossible to see any successful person ever desiring to decline; because they are always very conscious of what it took them to get there. Every millionaire, for instance, has a secret, forming a past for him or her. In like manner, always try to protect your past! However, a great many persons discuss theirs as so consistently unconditionally as to even do it on the streets, let alone while with their companions. You see? You know what? You're simply wrecking and/or duplicating your success key. Rather, learn to treasure and cover your past. If, however, you must discuss it, it's got to be done diplomatically; because others will never detail theirs to you. Otherwise, it implies that you don't value yourself. You know why? It's because your past is your duplicate, helping you to work out your original destiny.

Chapter Two

The Difference between the Past and the Future

Although the past is as much naturally inter-wound with the future as is the other to the one, slightly a differentiating instrument is their hybrid.

Despite how indisputably related are two elements, for instance, there must exist another element trying to erect something distinctive in-between. Despite how almost of the same meaning are two English words, for instance, they are still considerably different in meanings. In like manner, despite how inter-wound and/or inter-married with each are the past and the future, there still exists a difference between them. What is that difference? It is your *current future*. However, a great many persons call it *present*.

Although wrong or mistaken not is he who calls it *present* using a *literal* eye, it is indisputably wrong when using a *logical* eye. Why? It is because the word *present* is generic - it is accessible to all, in its sense, whereas the word *future* is logical – it is individually determined. How? The way one understands a thing is different from the way another does. And because success is inextricably tied to human existence, it takes a great degree of logicality to extract it, making it generally compulsory to be as much always logical in life as one can. You see? This is the reason why human existential *present* should no longer be called so. Rather, begin seeing it as your *current future*. And because human present is but tied to one of human great enemies – complacency, being sceptically analytical by all becomes mandatory. And because the ideal *current future* does not harbour such a human enemy, but rather an ignition device for more increase, we've got no other choice than to cluster this *current-future* philosophy.

Furthermore, human present is never ever desirous of more; it is usually with a view to compiling the already attained. You now understand that human present is analytically, practically determined; its fruitfulness or futility is based on how exactly you perceive it. This is what can make someone to retrogress in life. Once you feel satisfied with your current success level, relaxation comes on board; whereas if you try and not be content with it, no matter what, aspiration keeps playing or ruling. In a nutshell, therefore, one's current future is the time for one to analyze one's success pretty logically, in order to realize and aim at something greater. And so the difference between the past and the future is the all-known as *present*. This philosophy can mar one as much as it can also make one, because whereas it is partly acting as a linkage between your past and your future, it is also behaving like an *English synonym*. This is to say that, it also tries to form its own separate domain. And so if you can't link it to your next future, it will cause you so much damage. The key to doing this is determined by your logicality ability, by rather seeing it as your current future – the manifestation of your immediate past. Why? The word *present* gives a sense of separateness, isolation or solitude, whereas the philosophy *current future* gives a sense of genealogy, relativism or similarity. And for the fact that no right-thinking person would ever desire to get his or her past unlinked from his or her future, we've got to act rather wisely and logically. Know this: the word *present* is as much dynamic as the philosophy *current future*. How? If today is seen as your present, on the one hand, tomorrow will still be seen in the same way; likewise if it is seen as your current future, on the other hand. However, as we already know, they differ greatly in their effectiveness. The word *present* is *stagnancy-oriented*, whereas the word *future* is *activity-based*. And as such, if you sensitively adopt the latter philosophy, you are bound to progress unlimitedly. This is one of the reasons why a great many individuals now fail on a daily basis. You know why? Every success is given birth to by human actions, emanating from a series of *human-created* activities. And so if you're not activity-based, you're bound to lack and then diminish. Wow! In other words, the more the variety of activities, the more the different successes you attain. Nowadays, however, a great many individuals don't seem to do a variety of works anymore, whereas their expectations are very many. Sincerely speaking, no entrepreneur has a single target, as far as their vision is concerned. You know how? They don't ever have the mentality of, say, there exists a present, even the literal one. Therefore they work as much timelessly as they can. Just bear in mind that once the tenor of your *present* changes negatively, you will certainly have secured a horrible past. But it is this current-future philosophy that can make you conscious enough to maintain *it*. The difference between your past and your future would rather yield in your memory greater expectations, instead of relaxation. Logically speaking, this *difference* is but a period of new positive perceptions about one's existence. And one sure thing is the fact that once you can analyze your current future appropriately, your future must be greater.

As we are talking about the difference between one's past and one's future, what exactly do you think is here meant? Well, if you look at a coin very sceptically, you will find that where separates both sides is rather spitting. This is exactly how imperceptibly separated are the human past and the future. They are not to be weighed either beyond or below their natural effects, which is the reason why the past usually soon becomes as much the future as well as the future another/a new past. They act based on their natural timing. And so by the time one loses the timing, one will have caused oneself so great a loss. Time waits for no one, remember? This is the reason why we've got not to relax insensitively; you know what I mean. In relation to that, it is particularly, surprisingly pitiable to see a yet-to-be-financially-stable person rather finding it funny and appealing to ensure that the previous earning is exhausted before making for another. No, life is obviously not to be lived in such a fashion! You know what? Once you live in such a way, you're simply acting based on the complacency-oriented philosophy. Remember, human present is naturally fleeting, which is the reason why you don't have to call it a *present*. Always try to maximize the use of your current future! By the time you are trying to maximize it, you are going to have discovered whether or not it is sufficient. To buttress the coin illustration, anything dropped onto the boundary of a coin is naturally bound to spill over immediately onto either side. If so, why do you think or take your present for a stage of relaxation? If you see it as a current future, you are liable to discover if it is somewhat *ill*. The difference between the past and the future is caused by the period when a dual birth should be given. How? If you don't manage your current future well, you will have any longer neither a past nor a future. This is to say that this difference is caused by one's current future - to have to give birth to both another future and a new past. In other words, by the time one mesmerizes this period, one will have caused oneself not only a future damage, but also an immediate one. In essence, the possibility that one will experience both another future and a new past is as much tied to one's logicality practical ability as one's future cannot be isolated from one's past. This is the reason we must not allow our current future to yield any negativity. For instance, if one continually sleeps when others are busy working, one will certainly realize to have created for oneself so much backwardness. In like manner, if one fails to carry out this existential logicality analysis when it's still due, one definitely gets eluded by a very next-to-door success opportunity. In other words, so long as the clock keeps ticking without a single break, so tireless is one's effort required, once one is yet alive, working and hoping for more.

Chapter Three

The Hybrid of the Past and the Future

Anything without a bi-product is liable to exist no longer some day, because its life source is single.

As the major aim of every right-thinking father, be him successful or unsuccessful, is but to strive for a child-successor, so also very proud of is the hybrid of the past and the future. The bi-products of most bombs are practically capable of reproducing whole new ones. The bi-product of a cassava stem is not only capable of germinating on its own, but also reproducing a whole new stem. The bi-product (the seed) of an orange fruit is not only capable of germinating on its own, but also yielding several whole new fruits, to cite but a few examples. This is the reason why one's current future is capable of reproducing not only another whole new future, but also a whole new past, keeping one's existence going. And so our current future is as very important to our existence as to have to ensure that it performs its core or primary duty. Human current future is not something to be neglected; it is something that must be consciously, properly managed. It requires a great deal of help from us, such as monitoring, trimming and supporting it, so as to enable it to perform its dual function. In other words, it needs a great deal of concentration from us. Any current future that is not well handled is liable to diminish and finally vanish with its precious seeds. Don't joke with your current future! However, I've seen and also heard of a great many successful individuals who abruptly depreciated financially fatally as to no longer be able to regain their previous financial balance. This is usually caused by negligence. How? It is because it's not just attaining an appreciable success level that matters in life; it is maintaining and boosting it up. It is just like the case of someone being given a cute little dog to train. If one fails in such course, one fails not only in training and/or growing it, but also in improving its beauty. In like manner, every current future is as much deserving of the highest level of caring and trimming as does any cute little dog. Additionally, this of the little-old lady is a very brilliant and suitable example to our discourse. She was being given a cute little dog to rear. Although she tried the best she could in rearing it, she was almost exhausting all her resources on it. Owing to the obvious unbearable spending, she began complaining very bitterly, regardless of her still cherishing the puppy. One day she had a very musing thought to have to entrust it to one of her aunts. She said: *aunt, please, do help me take care of my little pet; I do no longer have the financial ability enough to take good care of it, but I still cherish it. Please try and do me this favour. I wouldn't want anything to happen to it! Thank you.* Based on her indisputable seriousness and persistence, her aunt collected the pet, trained it very appreciably, until she regained her financial ability and had to go back for it. You see? Once a thing is truly cherished, it certainly turns out rather reasonable to protect it to the end. From the above story, we discovered that the owner of the cute puppy was sensitive enough to be able to protect not only the growth and the survival of the puppy, but also its beauty. In like manner, how much do you cherish your (own) current future (the hybrid of your past and your future)? Sincerely speaking, spending the whole of your over-the-years earning doesn't depict that you cherish your success - it's rather by helping it to spread its fibres. That is it! Mere attaining a hen, for instance, does not guarantee your benefit from it - you're going to have to try enough to enable it to lay its precious eggs for you. Ok, why do poultry farmers often look forward to achieving the eggs of their hens? You see? This is the reason why, in like manner, we're all going to need to try enough in working out our current future, until we achieve its *precious eggs*.

However, many people are good only at making their current future yield for them a manageable future, but alongside it a horrible past. Once the future is manageable, the past is entirely of no worth. You know why? Whereas you can still merge the particles of your disintegrated future and achieve something sort of manageable, the past can no longer be attended to. Still, you cannot do away with it. It's only a good past that usually works as though it were the future, because of its overwhelming, positive flexibility, thereby becoming clearly suitable to your future. Otherwise, instead of becoming supportive of one's future, it mars it, rendering one to have to start all over. In essence, it is no ideal for one to indulge in some shady deeds today, simply because one cherishes one's tomorrow. It is absolutely wrong! What one is simply doing is insensitively deracinating one's harvest. Let's consider this: if one intends killing or taking possession of a snake alive, one's got not trample upon or grapple its tail; otherwise, one will rather become a victim of one's intention. Thus, one is going to have to target the head. In like manner, don't think you can successfully destroy your past and yet attain a good or positive future. It's absolutely impossible! But if you can sensitively, morally focus on your future without wounding, let alone destroying, your past, your target is genuinely sure. This is what makes human current future often the most logical period to handle. Similarly, it's worth sharing this of the politician, who had successfully manoeuvred his way into power, by wasting several other destinies (souls). Unfortunately, when the day of reckoning emerged, he was not only impeached, but also annihilated. You see? Your past is the spokesman of your future (success). Therefore, at this juncture, it is ideal for us to try as much to strive for the attainment of a good past as we should the future. Your destiny lies in your hands!

Additionally, don't base your destiny on the principle of envy or hatred. Rather, learn to be yourself, by practicing your own skills and technical know-how, to attain your own success. Remember, your future is as much embodied in your today as is your past. Learn to do good by favouring and supporting others, and you will surely climb higher. The past is the most *incorruptible judge.* How? It is because it outlines and promulgates every bit of one's past deeds. And if our past is embodied in our today, why, then, should we not be careful of the kind of what we do to others on a daily basis? Think about this. There is no how nature will desert you if you truly base your target on the right philosophy. Don't succeed against others, but among them. Sincerely speaking, anything that is successfully done and/ or attained against the precious law of living does not usually last. Instead of increasing one, it retards one into eternal retrogression. This is the reason why one should endeavour one's target is genuine. In other words, once one sensitively bases it on the-kind-of-what-everyone-should-do principle, today, one's future will certainly not experience any unexpected condemnation, tomorrow. Additionally, the hybrid of the past and the future is like the lingua franca that systematically brings about the coalition of different national ethnic groups. This is but the reason why we've all got to be extremely sensitive of how we make this hybrid to carry out its core purpose. Otherwise, it will still look like some nations with common existing languages but yet struggling to communicate. Thus, it needs to be directed, nurtured and properly monitored. It is like the case of a growing flower, which once it grows beyond the level that brings about or maintains its beauty, not only will its core purpose have been lost, but also constituted nuisance. In essence, whatever that is a hybrid is not to act beyond its core purpose; otherwise, it will ruin its *parents*. Therefore the hybrid of the past and the future is only but to have to help bring forth not only a new future, but also a very remarkable past. And the only way to do this, as human beings, is to learn to act as much very cautiously on a daily basis as we truly cherish our existence. Furthermore, the hybrid of your past and your future is the glory of your existence on earth. Therefore always maintain its gloriousness. The stubbornness of a child, for instance, is usually attributed to his/her parents; likewise if he or she is obedient to all. In like manner, the wrongness or awkwardness of the hybrid of the past and the future is obviously traceable to its parents. And so if you truly cherish your existence, don't allow that to occur, because everything boils down to your essence. To avoid something contrary, always endeavour to regulate the growth of the hybrid of your past and your future from exceeding its natural circumference. How? It is by always thinking, acting and judging happenings based on the right principles, and never on the wrong ones. Exactly!

Chapter Four

The relevance of the past to the future

Anything that is not of relevance is as much of
no desire as any leftover.

It is because the sky is practically relevant to the earth that it usually relieves it with precipitation. It is because the eye is obviously useful to the brain that it is usually quickened whenever there is any alertness tendency. It is because of how practically useful is water to plants that they can't survive, let alone yield any fruits, without it. It is because of how impressively useful are the human bowels to the tummy that excretion cannot take place without the former. It is because of how divinely germane is food to *man* that none can exist without it. It is because of how indisputably indispensable is the gill to the fish that they could never have existed under the water without it, to state but a few. This is the reason why if something must be useful, it must be pretty relevant in its sense. It is therefore evident that whatever that does not obey the natural principle of relevance is bound not to be useful, constituting nuisance, in the entirety of its existence. Similarly, for one to be useful and then peaceful in life, one is going to have to try as much to be pretty relevant in every facet of life as one can. And one can never be useful without by always practicing what is right. In relation to our discourse, therefore, for one's past to be relevant and then useful to one's future, one has to make it right. In other words, one must base it on the right ideal. This is to say that one's past may have been based on some irrelevant, illegal ideal, yesterday, only for one's future to realize this and then begin to head in a different, relevant direction, today. You see? In that case, what could one do? You know what? Both would certainly not merge. This is the reason why we've got to base our past on the generally legal, relevant ideal of living - the principle of morality and justice. Once the past cannot clasp well with the future, both become just as much so irrelevant and then rebellious as are usually evident of two opposing sides of magnet. And once this happens, they begin to act like two warring brothers, constituting one kind of nuisance or the other. It's here worth surmising that a great many individuals, however, suffer or struggle today because of the strong disagree existing between their past and their future. And this disagree would always be effective because it is usually being prompted by the elderly (the past) against the younger (the future). How? An author unveils, saying: *Today is the father of tomorrow.* Therefore the past is not only elderly to the future, but also a father. And also if one's earthly father says *no!* to his child's action, what authority has the child to act contrarily to what is being instructed or ordered by his father? It takes only a prodigal son to act otherwise. In like manner, one should not behead the other today and expect his or her own head to be spared tomorrow. You know what that means? It's just like the case of one who throws stones against the other's glass house, whereas the former also lives in a house of same. In this case, what kind of reaction would you expect from the other? It is a retaliation of the same act, of course. No matter how one fortifies one's future against one's past, the former will still be overpowered by the latter. Similarly, don't fight with or injure your father and then run away from the house; he will certainly know where exactly to which you must have escaped. Ok if one's father curses one, what usually befalls the cursed? Therefore, don't let your past say otherwise to your future.

In a nutshell, always endeavour your past is greatly relevant to your future. If both speak in one voice, they will be harmonious and then relevant to each other. But if either's tone is different from the other's, there is a serious problem. And so the game of the past and the future is obviously based on the principle of *plumbing*. As a bricklayer, if you fail to carry out accurate plumbing while laying your bricks, your walls are bound to collapse, leading to a precious effort entirely wasted. In like manner, as a future-inclined person walking towards attaining a better living, try the best you can not to juxtapose your past and your future. And so proper and/or accurate plumbing should be done. Additionally, why the principle of the past and not that of the future should be acted based on is because the former usually gives birth to the latter. Although, technically, they are apparently simultaneous in their evolvement, the past is still the backbone of the future. Thus, for one's future to be accredited in any way, one's past must first be consulted. Practically, for instance, declaring someone as the best footballer of the year is never ever based on fortuitousness; it is usually determined by the person's overwhelming past records. Therefore if the credibility of the future is determined by the past, of what effect, then, is the former without the latter? The past must be relevant to the future!

In essence, the kind of what one does today is exactly what manifests tomorrow. However, a great many people always rejoice, saying: *My future will be greater!* while they are yet to work on it. Your future is embodied in your current future; so begin working on it now. The outcome of every today's work is that which forms and/or shapes your future. Let me tell you something: in a very logical manner, your next future also manifests in your current future; but it's tactically based on human actions. How? For instance, if one works in the morning and gets paid by nightfall that same day, that's practically the outcome of one's morning action(s). Therefore if one becomes a little more financially fitter by evening than one was in the morning, one's situation or experience has improved for better, which practically makes one's morning period a past to one's evening period. With this understanding, how far do you think your future is from your past? Actually, they are embodied in everything we do at every waking moment. Contrarily, if one's former action or deed is an antithesis of the latter, one may even get killed or imprisoned for it; a vivid display of the irrelevance of one's past to one's future. If, however, one does something morally or legally acceptable in the morning, one may even get rewarded for it before evening. This is the relevance of one's past to one's future. With all this, it's evident that our future is much nearer to our past than we could ever imagine. Do good today, to live well tomorrow! And so the purpose of this chapter is to unveil to us what must be done to attain a blameless or irreprehensible future. Don't make your today speak otherwise against your tomorrow! Invest right today, to harvest equally right tomorrow. Don't try to manipulate, because nature is immutable. Live justifiably today, to reap equally justifiably tomorrow. Remember, your tomorrow is your hope. Don't mesmerize it! Overall, the more the relevance of your past, the better the allegiance of your future! Think big, but certainly not with evil.

Chapter Five

Do We Ever Have a Present?

Any relaxation without aspiration is liable to cause depreciation and then serious retrogression.

In the history of every human existence, there is always an I-have-arrived period, usually based on some generic mentality that has now pervaded the ultimate logical reasoning of a great many individuals. Naturally, there is absolutely nothing wrong with such ideal, but the only case is how it is being perceived and then practiced. It's just like the case of one who idealizes burning his or her first car for the second. This kind of act is not only irrational, but also foolishly barbaric. Similarly, why is it indisputably not ideal for one to have to kill the first-born for the second? Oops! You know what? This would not only be crazy, but also spiritually perilous and penal. Ok why also do people not ever deem it fit burning down or demolishing the first of one's buildings for the second, except that which is not only already outmoded, but also rickety-old? Therefore if we so value things like these, why don't we value our existence as much? That is the question! This is because our existence is not only our pride, but also the obvious reason why other things can be valued. In relation to our discourse, therefore, the issue of whether or not a human will live satisfactorily long is dependent on how one conceives one's *present*. And so the question is, how do we conceive the human present? Actually, this phenomenon has denied a great many human existences not only a lot more treasures to come, but also the ability to conceive more of life and then live longer. This then results to why we've got not to think we have a particular present, but that every time in the life of every human existence is a working and/or helping-the-current-future present, and that also which is rather far from relaxation and overt or beyond-the-ordinary merriment. This is the reason why, logically, we do not have to act based on the philosophy of the kind of present that has marred the logical and success reasoning of a great many for ages. And the ignorance of this is the reason why many are rather prodigal in nature – by usually lavishing their last and most earning, and then retrogress. Similarly, there was this vibrant and promising young man who was rather misfortunate to have been too early acquainted with poverty. However, as God would have it, he tried and managed to sell off his only left-behind-by-my-father plot of land for a very huge sum of money. Guess what he did with it all! He instead organized a big bash and then invited all his far-and-near friends to come drink in celebration with him, with the overwhelming satisfaction that he had arrived. You know what? Sooner than later, he began regretting to have ever been so stupid and prodigal, and that he should have invested the whole money in something clearly lucrative. What kind of lesson did we learn from the above story? The foregoing makes us to realize that once one insensitively acts based on the I-have-arrived principle, one surely retrogresses. And this retrogression is inextricably tied to the philosophy of the belief that human beings do have a *present*. Similar of this simple logic is indisputably evident of the kind of what usually befalls a great many insensitive individuals in every first month of the year – January, as a result of their having to have lavished to the last kobo of their from-the-first-to-the-last-month-of-the-year savings. Hmmm, this is absolutely wrong! You know what? You are simply over stretching the productiveness of your existence, instead of helping it. No, this is no ideal! Although it's no wrong for one to celebrate one's success, especially in such celebration-based seasons, it becomes almost a crime when one turns it wrong-side-up. You know what? Whatever makes one to regret in any way is outright out of the game of morality and rationality, resulting to the question, *what kind of thing is this?* from eye-witnesses. In other words, *too much of everything is bad*, as it is commonly known. With all this, do we really have a present? Whereas literally we do, we logically absolutely don't. This is what should now be our kind of reasoning, to be able to trim and maintain our existence in an appropriate fashion.

Furthermore, why a great many also struggle is either because of not investing in something really lucrative or because of just focusing on one thing that is logically not worth relying on. This is to say that human profits or benefits are supposed to be realized as much unconditionally consistently as the human logical present is consistent. However, many always say in extreme satisfaction: *I have made so much money!* Although you may have made a lot of money, how sure are you that you have made the most? That's if it is even possible to make the most money. Let me tell you something: making money is one thing, but properly managing it to be substantial or tangible is another. This is because the world is spherical, likewise its logicality. Similarly, this is the reason why the world of science is not static but dynamic, moving very technically along with the change of the logicality of nature. This is, however, the reason why a great many nations are not inventive; because they are not speedily or radically scientific enough to beat the spherical nature of the world and then grab and practice its modern logicality. This is because nature itself doesn't have a particular present – everything is usually geared very speedily towards the manifestation of its divine, mysterious methodology. Therefore if nature itself does not idealize giving room for complacency and relaxation, how much more we that are controlled and manipulated by the selfsame nature? This is the reason why we have to reason and act like nature at all times. In a nutshell, anyone who is not successful is logically not nature-bound. And so he or she is not controlled by nature; because of not obeying and acting like her (nature). And if nature is successful, how could anyone be financially a cast-off? It wouldn't be possible, of course! Therefore don't be lazy, but try and be cleverly crazy in your success reasoning! In this way, circumstances and failures will not come any nearer, let alone defocusing you. Let me tell you something: the reason why a lot of nations are not inventive is clearly owing to great, consistent and technical thinkers lacking. One of my poems *What Kills a Nation* is very explicit in its assertion on this. Thus, the more one thinks, the better the working on one's status. Endeavour to perceive your present as much in your thinking time as is usually done in your non-thinking time. This is the only way you can logically beat down the destructive nature of complacency. Your present is as much now as any time else. This is the way you can successfully convert your literal present into a greater future. Once you can do this, your greater future and your more remarkable past are sure! Do you want this? Then think about it.

Chapter Six

When Exactly Do We Have a future?

Any future without good or proper functioning
is a friction.

Many are futureless because they are visionless, which usually leads to unsuccessfulness. However, those who are diligently future-inclined always enjoy their future at last. This is to say that one's future is inextricably tied to the wheels of one's vision, immutably dragged along with it to the place of manifestation. This is the reason why every good future cannot be realized anyhow. On the contrary, many always feel the human future is tied to a particular season for its manifestation to be realized. No. It is and can only be geared and made manifest by one's vision. This implies that if one's vision is set or targeted to manifest in several years ahead, so also will it be the manifestation of one's future. Furthermore, one's future can be as equally far as it is near. How? This now calls for the application of our human logicality ability; that which revealingly emphasizes that the manifestation of one's future is logically, individually determined. In this way, one's future can either be now, immediately after now, or far after now. And so we can't say it all, yet. But one so sure thing is that any future that is not conceived to be in existence already is bound to run out of validity and then wear off – you know what that means. And so, in relation to our discourse, any future that needs continuous or progressive validity is but to have to be conceived right and logically dependably well. If, however, one fails to maintain the validity of one's future – that which is usually responsible for the right manifestation, one's future is bound to be fruitless. The only way one can successfully maintain the validity of one's future is to believe and then be subconscious of the fact that the human future is continuous. How? This now redirects us to knowing the hidden emphasis behind the concept of this chapter.

In a nutshell, the emphasis behind the concept of this chapter is inextricably tied to the logical understanding that one's future is only achievable by one's belief. Although, generally, the human future is existentially determined, it is apparently more individually determined; because the validity and effectiveness of one's future is overwhelmingly prompted and/or pioneered by one's perception about one's existence, in particular. This is the reason why once people conceive and believe themselves as failures, they always fail; because one's conception or belief about oneself is what usually brings about one's ability that is either to cause failure or success. In like manner, one's future can either be positively or negatively effective, as a result of one's conception and belief about one's own destiny. In other words, one's conception and belief about oneself or destiny is to be absolutely positive; otherwise it certainly turns out negative. You know why? Negativity and positivity are like two sides of a coin, making it either the one or the other. This is the reason why the merriment of a few individuals is uninterruptedly unending, whereas a great many experience it once in several seasons. This is as a result of how they conceive and believe the human future operates. To digress a little, this is also one of the reasons why a great many believe their exist witches and wizards hunting them daily; because, owing to their own belief, their future is not consistently manifest in a positively productive way, resulting to poverty, hardship and then the belief in spiritual hindrances. However, those who are naturally successful, based on their divine logical thinking understanding, live millions of miles away from the belief of, say, there are witches and wizards troubling and hindering people's successes daily. You see? This kind of thinking is the only thing worth applying in your belief about your existence. And so this chapter stipulates that the manifestation of one's future is clearly dependent on one's belief. But, generally, the human future is always, but imperceptibly changing in time and period. Thus, it does this to keep abreast with the ever spherical nature of the world's existence, in general. This is the reason why if your thinking ability is not in equivalence with that of your future, it will not only outrun you, but also desert your existence; the reason life itself is dynamic. If you fail to reason in line with the velocity of the changeability of your unfailing future, which walks hand in hand with nature, the true manifestation of your future will not only leave you behind, but also deny you all its success packages like a water tide, bringing about the experience of emptiness or penury.

This therefore implies that one's future can never be several years ahead, as many always feel. No! One's future is as much now, after now, as it can be much later. It is this understanding that can enable you to approach your future right. This is clearly however of a great many individuals who are already in their future but thinking it's yet several years ahead. Once one is still this ignorant of the emergence of one's future, one can never enjoy the good of it. This is clearly like if you have a car but unfortunately do not know how to drive it. In like manner, if you don't drive your future right, you will not only run into something and disfigure it, but also lose its essence – you know what that means. Actually, this usually befalls only those who never worked for or towards their future. Is there any true farmer who could be as so unconscious of his suffering as to not knowing when his crops are due for harvest? I doubt. In other words, if one truly works on or towards one's future, the manifestation of one's future is bound to be duly noticed and properly managed, and not damaged. And so the human future is as much not to delay itself up for any reason as is time itself. Thus, we've got to study our future. This makes it necessary imbibing the fact that there exists a current future, as earlier discussed in the preceding chapters. Once this principle is your yardstick, the emergence of your future can never take you unawares, let alone outrunning you. And so this *future thing* is a philosophy on its own that requires another whole philosophy to understand it, and then approach it right.

Furthermore, it is, however, a principle that does not obey any wrong principle; because it is a divine thing. Thus, basing its study on any wrong principle is what usually fails many. And so if one is evil in one's actions, for instance, one can never achieve anything good from one's future. Do you know why? This is because the human future *believes* in rewarding one in accordance with one's deeds, and not giving out something based on what was never desired and/or practiced by one. In other words, do good always, to make your future greatly *friendly* to you and then keep you *fully updated* about the manifestation of the things you desire in life. If truly you believe doing the right thing is the sole principle and, probably, your current future is not doing well, try work towards attaining a greater one, by putting more effort, as *heaven* helps you. You cannot change your future, but you can change your strategy. And so if your current future is not good enough, use another strategy, to make it better off or more productive. And the only thing you need to do is to analyze it in the proper logical manner. But remember, the number of commodities stocked in a warehouse determines how much is bound to be realized after the total sale is carried out. Therefore if your future is not productive enough, see yourself as being responsible for it. And so learn to speak and to do good always into your future. Your future requires positively wonderful prophecies from you, and certainly not blasphemies. If one doesn't help direct one's yam-shoot, for instance, by pinning a stick to it, it is bound to stray off shoot and, then, lose its essence. And so help your today's future, in order to get duplicated from it another whole new, more productive future for you, tomorrow. Your future is as much today as it is tomorrow. Therefore, don't joke over it! Additionally, this implies that you can help better off your future, but you cannot eliminate it. It must come, and so you must be ready for it. However, when your future may not/is bound not to obey you is when you try to *pollute* it with some wrong ideal. And so like two inseparable friends are you and your future, if only you know and respect each other's likes and dislikes!

Chapter Seven

What Usually Brings about the Past?

For the fact that every human being is a hybrid of two opposite but divinely of-one-Father existences does not, and cannot, bring about any invalidation in one way or the other by the one against the other. Rather, the one remains petted, nurtured, fed, trained, protected and overly provided for by the other at all times.

Why every human being has an anus is for excretion's sake. This is an obviously explicit illustration to enable us to know, without much cracking of brains, why the human past is doubtless inevitable to every human being. Conversely, a great many existences are still millions of miles away from the reason why the human past is, why it should be, and what usually brings about it; thereby even contributing to its ruin. This is because if one knows the function and/or usefulness of a thing, for instance, one certainly helps it to achieve its purpose. On the contrary, if one does not know the worth of a thing, one rather mars it. Therefore, in relation to our discourse, how much of worth do you think your past is? It is having got a very suitable answer to the above question that one can appropriately help in securing a good past for oneself. After this, one may then think of what usually brings about a good past. It is very simple! How? The past is precious, and so it should be worked towards as such. Furthermore, every good past is but expected to evolve like one's next future, both powered by one's current future. In other words, the current future should as much be able to bring about a good past as its next future. But the question is, how can this be successfully done? Well, it all depends on the way of life of the existence involved. Napoleon reveals that *if a man is right, his world will be right.* On this note, it is obvious that every wrong past created is doubtless as a result of the life style of the individual involved. Therefore if your existence is wrong, your *world* is equally wrong and pretty damaged. The reason is because a great many rather desire to live like animals, whereas the human species is that which should be promoted always with rational, moral deeds. Once one fails to do this, one's essence becomes confused; unless one were from another species. And so you should not dare disgrace your entity and yet expect any good from *nature*. Frankly speaking, this is the reason why a great many seem naturally, unproductively abandoned; because of their sabotaging deeds against their identity – the human species. You know what? Nature itself would not only desert such an existence, but also look forward to rendering him or her worthless. Therefore if one is not living right on a daily basis, one is simply and/or unconsciously accumulating the incurable wrath of nature upon oneself.

But as those who rather look forward to attaining a good past, we've got to be extremely conscious of our target. The reason is because whatever that is not being based on a clear, conscious act or intention is that which is rather pioneered by fortuitousness, which is very likely to lead to some severely destructive, unacceptable result. Why? It's because whether or not one is conscious of the evolvement of one's past, one's past must come. In that case, it is clearly compulsory for one to work on and direct it. In a nutshell, what usually brings about the past is the effectiveness of one's existence, be it positive or negative. This is the reason why everyone is bound to have a past, except one who leaves no longer. Therefore, the daily deeds of an individual are what make up his or her past. And so living should be viewed like the art of driving a car: if one is conscious of it enough to maintain one's car steering in the right/customary sense, one's car tyres will not only be straight enough to attain a very good and enjoyable balance for the car, but also create a pretty beautiful, plausibly natural sensation in the mind as to how characteristically disciplined the driver must have been in the course of the driving. In like manner, for one to be able to create not only a good but also enjoyable past, one is going to have to control, very sensibly, every bit of one's daily deeds. This is to say that if one does otherwise, one's past is bound to be like the macabre scenes usually created by the destructive, unfriendly weapons of warring soldiers. You know why? It's simply because human deeds are like weapons, but those which are only reasonable when one is logical and moral enough to make them function right. Practically, it is also like the case of one who possesses a knife: if one is logical and moral enough to use it to slice but only those things that are fruity or eatable, it will not only have served its primary purpose, but also created a unique, beautiful culture of the use of it. On the other hand, if it is used to pierce someone, its essence is therefore lost. You see? So also is the human deed – the reason why we should know when, where, why and how to act. Once you know this, your wonderfully beautiful past is sure!

Have you ever analyzed an acre of cultivated corns, for instance? Its complete growth is usually traceable to the rigorous, commendable effort of the farmer. This now brings about the simple understanding that living is like cultivating – that whose evidence is normally based on time. Thus, one's overall effort (in working on oneself) is usually known to all. One mysterious thing about the human past is that it's not like one's son whom can possibly be disowned, for any reason, and it may be acceptable; it is something that is inextricably tied to the human existence. In that case, would you rather die? No! That's why we've all got to act right always. Let me tell you something: if someone puts on a shoe and begins striding, it is the design beneath it that is bound to tell the kind of what the person has on (whether it is a flat or soled shoe), continuing in accordance with the pace of the movement of the individual. Therefore if the human past is similar to this, the longer of one's earthly stay, the longer his or her past, too. And as such, no one can run away from, neither deny, his past! And so the only way to be right is to live right. Additionally, working on the past is like having an urn to fill: the more you fill it, the longer it sustains you. This then gives the understanding that why a great many individuals are suffering, today, is simply because they weren't sensitive and future-inclined enough to have filled their urns to the brims, yesterday. This is to say that the more elastic your past is, the longer your future will be, until it may have to be re-ignited. No doubt. Not until one realizes this, living comfortably will always seem a dogfight. And so think right today! Furthermore, human deeds are like the bricks laid in setting up a building. Thus, one's deeds are the bricks for setting up a good past for oneself. Therefore, how well mixed are your existential bricks? If only we were conscious of this fact, we could never be taken unawares by circumstances, which usually lead to the truncation of a lot of distinctive visions. Why? It is simply because one's existential bricks are what set up the building that brings about one's essence, on earth. However, a great many have failed utterly in maintaining their earthly, individual purposes. Hmmm! Nevertheless, consciousness is the sole key to regaining and maintaining one's lost existence. It's therefore not late yet!

Chapter Eight

How Can One Make and Maintain a Good past?

The base of a building determines how long will be the stay of that building.

Human existence is channelled towards the past – the base. This is because living is but that which is powered by the past. And so human existence's sustainability, or source of livelihood, is past-determined. This is to say that every natural living is the manifestation of the past. In other words, although life may still be without a good past, the real sense of it is absent. This is what makes it natural to have to imbibe and practise the making of a good past based on its divine principle – the act of being absolutely conscious of what we do on a daily basis, to be moral and justifiable enough in life. Therefore one might ask: how can one make and maintain a good past? Well, this chapter is basically of two parts: first - making; second - maintaining. The one is as essentially inevitable as the other, reason being that if you destroy or neglect the one, you automatically, unconsciously do same to the other. You know why? This is because it is rather natural as to the fact that a thing maintained is a thing already achieved, just as a thing achieved is that which is maintained. Explicitly, therefore, if an achiever eventually becomes neglectful to why he should maintain his achievement, he suddenly turns a has-been (and you know what that means). You know what? Even more horrible is when one eventually turns a has-been. And being a has-been is often suggestive of so many of both well-conceived and misconceived thoughts. And so it's what should be avoided as much as possible! Two things are liable to cause this: either relaxation or ill-foundation. Having known this, it is therefore paramount to know how to *make* a good past.

Making a good past is as simple as it can be difficult. The reason is because it is something that cannot be done in another way round. It is fixed. Why? The reason is because the human past is nature-bound, which implies that it is subject to the law of nature. In other words, it cannot be unnatural as to be able to take the shape of how it was not originally made by one. Understood?

Now, to make it plainer, it means that how one makes it is precisely the fashion in which it evolves. If one makes one's past horrible, it equally emerges horrible. On this note, therefore, we've got to take an especial, conscious view on how our various pasts should be (made). Frankly speaking, therefore, what makes one's past is the overall existence fashion of the individual involved. And so since it is natural that none can give what one does not possess, it's then believable that the scrambled past of an individual is caused by his or her own manner of existence. Now let's consider this: I want you to see it believable that we make our pasts. How, you might ask? Good. This is indisputable as to the sense that your living person is what brings to memory your past. Without your being alive, your past is nowhere. Moreover, someone else's past cannot be attributed to another. So also it is when making a past – the one cannot make it for the other. As it was being revealed much earlier that making a past is as much simple as it can be difficult, it is individually and/or character-determined. This means that not until one sees oneself as one's past can such an individual ever make a good past. In other words, you are yourself your past! You make your past – either horribly or appreciably – by the consistency of the fashion in which you live on a daily basis; which now reveals that the human past lives in us.

Furthermore, once you fail to see yourself as your past, you wreck your past, as well as yourself. Always endeavour to work on your person in relation to the attainment of your desired kind of past. If people know you as a daily nuisance, your past is equally as you are – and it cannot *say* otherwise. Therefore, your past is the faithful manifestation of your daily actions – the immediate manifestation of your personality. Isn't it? Well, unfortunately, this is the reason why a great many individuals have failed in life. To be more directly logical, is not the human past abstract, or is it visible as to be able to caution and direct it like can be done an individual? No, of course. It is immutably abstract in nature. Someone can commit homicide, today, and eventually get repented of it, tomorrow. Although repentance is declarable, commission is indelible. In other words, the declaration of one's repentance of a sin cannot deface the effect of the illegal commission by one. And so the past is the faithful *recording* of one's existence. And why a great many individuals are usually disqualified from being a member of the *world of greatness* is but because of the kind of recording that is got in stock of them. Once the recording of you speaks evil, that divine world of greatness rejects you immediately. The world of greatness is the world of success, honour and abundance. This is to say that if you are not doing well in life, your past is faulty. Check it up now! Conversely, a lot of people are, at the same time, fond of manoeuvring their way into this world. No doubt. Although one can successfully do that, nature still fishes one out and punishes him or her accordingly, no matter how long it may take. There are several ways to get into this world: one – by doing things individually; second – by doing things as a group or organization; third – by doing things as a people's leader; and four – by being to cater the interest of one's nation. By this we mean that in whichever area you find yourself doing one thing or the other, provided that it is right, you are a sure candidate of that world. And so it is not designed for any particular way. This is the reason why once the world of an individual is justifiable enough, it can successfully merge with the world of greatness (and you what that means).

In a nutshell, just bear in mind that the way you live either makes or mars your past. And remember, without a good past, the future is baseless; because the past is the *base* of the future – the *building*. Wow! You see? The past is now even almost more important than the future, if not that the other is the practical essence of the one. Hmmm! Additionally, this therefore reveals that if you daily caution your personal excesses as regards morality and justice, your past is surely productively presentable. Therefore you can no longer blame your past; because you are the past yourself.

This is reminiscent of the habit of many corrupt leaders or representatives out there. If the highest authority gives them an instruction to implement some strategy on how to tackle and/or eradicate corruption from a people, for instance, it is often a dogfight for them to even think about it as they are themselves corrupt. So how can you any longer blame or criticize your past when you are yourself no upright and yourself the selfsame past? Your past is an entity of you, just as your future of you. Why, then, do we usually claim a good future? We usually do this because we little understand that the future is but the past in the current. And that's why once your past is good your future is automatically good. To crown it all on this notion, the human past is the human in the physical – that is, the man walking and mingling with the others, daily. Why this notion is but to make us to realize that there's no other way by which we can make our pasts other than to be aware of this fact and then work on our distinct personalities; because we are but our walking pasts. Rather pitiable is the act of many who usually use their daily despicable deeds to truncate their records. The record held of you, to reiterate it, is the licence for the effectiveness of your past. Once one's record is unethical or damaged, one's future is as ineffectively useless as the likably presumable condition of a successful hunter-man but without a single tooth... This proverbially explains that the *teeth* of one's future is the record held generally of him or her; which implies that once that record is faulty, the teeth of one's future are gone(and you know what that means). This is the reason why it is as also very paramount to maintain one's past as is to make it. How can one maintain a good past? We find out.

The human past is as to be known as being highly delicate to maintain as the nature of an egg. How? By this is meant but its nature. Why liken this to an egg? If you have an egg in your palm, you usually do not have to busy your palm up with any other thing, regardless of how minor it might look, much less attaching it with something considered major – as you know it. Naturally, once you do so, consider the egg as an irreversible loss. Unfortunately, the absence of this simple understanding has failed many uncountable times. And so it is now but only a few individuals who can both make and also maintain a good past. Why? It is because the others are usually, characteristically fond of attaching and/or busying their palms up with other things – be them major or minor. And as *nature* would have it, that delicate shell that is the overall shield to the vulnerable nature of the sauce of an egg is indisputably symbolic of the nature of your past to your future. Realistically, you could have a mental picture of what the condition of the sauce of a broken egg is usually like.

It usually spills on the ground in aimlessness of an abrupt disaster, vividly suggestive of a plight of *fatherlessness*.

In a nutshell, the evidence of every human existence is this egg. Once one cracks the shell (the past), the sauce (the future) spills away into loss, wrecking yourself. And so beware that the *egg* of your existence is as delicate as the physical egg we all know. How does one crush this egg? One does this by either being hit-or-miss or greedily unethical. If you are careless, the consciousness of to have to protect your egg will be absent, just as you are bound to indulge yourself in one illegal practice or the other when you are greedy; but forgetting the fact that the egg of one's existence is one and only. Why a great many individuals are usually careless, in life, is owing to their lack of value for their existence. And why some are rather greedy is but because they think a good success is achievable only by dint of hard work or something. No! In this case, what constitutes a good success is the egg of the existence of an individual, implying that once you handle it in such a manner and it eventually gets crushed, you lose it all. So, live in accordance with the principle of *patience* and *carefulness*. In other words, if you are patient enough in life, you can be no greedy, just as you are bound not to crush your egg in carefulness. Additionally, the only way you can successfully avoid cracking the shell of your *sole* egg is by not placing it on a rough surface. By not placing it on a *rough surface* is meant, living in such a manner as to successfully avoid people speaking ill of you. This is to say that the more they embellish you with glowing remarks, the less delicate the shell of the egg of your existence becomes. On the other hand, the more the ills spoken of you by people, the more delicate the nature of your egg becomes. Unfortunately, the loss of this egg is usually fatal – once and for all. What is obtainable, then? It is the consciousness of the fact that no one shares with you his own egg! And you could imagine a hen without a single egg, for instance. But more unfortunately is the fact that to one human existence is assigned but only a single, lifetime egg! It means that once you crush yours, you are out of the *main* game, beginning to wander the sauce (your future) in the lamentation of some irreversible, had-I-known tone. Ok, is any cracked egg ever amendable? That's precisely the case! This makes it absolutely mandatory to protect it to the end. However, it is clearly apparent that a lot of people are still to understand what exactly it means to maintain or protect one's past, or even why they should. Yes. Well, it is not something difficult to accomplish, but it requires absolute consciousness. How? The only thing you need to begin is by believing – by accepting the fact that you and your daily actions constitute your past. Napoleon reveals in his book

Success through a Positive Mental Attitude, saying: *what your mind can conceive and believe, your mind can achieve it.* And so since it is evident and/or natural that whatever you do not believe cannot work for you, everything now depends on to have to believe what you desire or expect of life. In relation to our main notion, therefore, it's not until you believe and accept the fact that you are your past can you ever live right, in life. This is as so logical as to the fact that your uprightness embodies both the making and the maintaining of your past; only that the other (maintaining) requires some extra level of consistency from you. This is why it is usually pretty easier for more people to make than to maintain their pasts. Otherwise, there is no good past that is difficult to make. It is just like purchasing a car. Although a car may be considerably costly, affording it is not often the problem; it is maintaining it that matters. So, just as we usually deem it fit maintaining such or any desirable commodity, maintaining a good past is vividly a similar case to this. You know why? Your past is as even more of worth than such a desirable car as due to the fact that it is capable of making available for you whatever is your desire in life. How? I've witnessed, and also heard about, several cases of people trading their precious, century-old integrity for something merely of pleasure; forgetting that their just-traded integrity is the glorious essence of their existence. You see? That is exactly the case – a great many persons are still to know that which is rather the most important of all, in life. Furthermore, your integrity – that which constitutes your human essence and involves both the making and the maintaining of your good past, is your *treasure*. Whereas many always go after pleasure, they little know that pleasures of all kinds are equally embodied in treasures. Thus, you can never find a single treasure in a pleasure. Why, then, should we be ruining or wasting our precious lives over pleasures - things that don't pay? No! I go for treasures, instead! You see? We usually think pursuing material things is what makes available for us treasures, but not knowing that the treasures we seek here and there, injuring ourselves on a daily basis, are but readily available in us. Having known this, therefore, what should we do to make them come to light? Good! It's very simple. Once your outward person is but already a treasure of you, as a result of your life-style, all the world's pleasures – constituting every material thing – will engulf you forever! In other words, to make it plainer, everything you want is in you. This now reveals that it's not one's strength that provides one with one's expectations; it is one's life-style, which also makes it impossible to buy a good past. In fact, it is the number one thing I have ever seen so natural as to everyone to have to work for before attaining it. Once one tries to buy or forge it up in any way, *nature* certainly intervenes in due time. And so the only way one can truly merit/attain it is to work genuinely for it.

Once you have the ability to create and to maintain a good past for yourself, there is absolutely nothing else that may ever be difficult for you to work for/towards, attain and maintain. This is because *attainment* and *maintenance* are natural. In fact, they are human species-specific. This art started with creation. After God had created Adam, He gave him the power immediately to name and to safe-guard every other creature. You know what? Adam was only able to do that on account of the fact that the power was still very much fresh and active; because it was yet stainless. How? This is because Adam's past was still precious and appealing enough before God. And so, that time, he was completely able to control everything. However, once he did otherwise, even before God finally came to evacuate him and his wife from the precious, ethereal garden, his *past* had started haunting him. You see? In fact, it is one's scrambled past that disqualifies one from good things the most. Why the world is obviously difficult for us to live in, today, is owing to our various long, age-old scrambled pasts that we have rather decided to panel-beat and hobble along with on a daily basis, instead of simply carrying out an absolute overhaul on them once and for all. This reveals that committing sins is our greatest enemy. And so what do we do? It is as simple as just to have to try to be *selfless* in life as we can. Once you are selfless, you will often endeavour to keep yourself *stainless*. Why? It's because *stainlessness* is inextricably tied to *selflessness*, while *guiltiness* is in the same fashion tied to *greediness*. You know what? Adam automatically became guilty after he had decided to be greedy, and he got ostracized in due time. Have you seen it now that what we are saying is tied to our human species? This is why it is a bit difficult to do away with it. However, *nature* is ever looking for whom to reward according to his or her good deeds. Begin to think selflessly and become stainless, to make the world abidingly peaceful and joyous. In other words, the overall happiness and/or enjoyment of humans is naturally tied to how much stainless they are, in life. And the most painful part of it is that people, nowadays, think there is no other means by which one can be successful other than being corrupt – I mean joining them if you cannot beat them. This is wrong! Because it causes more harm than good. In like manner, if a canoe had had a leaking spot but would not be blocked or amended as soon as possible before the subsequent use of it, there is every tendency that its next experience from the leakage would be more perilous than the previous one. Therefore, once you think it doesn't matter and you eventually join the crowd, you've simply, unconsciously signed your death warrant. In fact, nobody ever thinks or struggles to attain a good reputation any longer. Tell me when not a single person is any longer thinking of doing the right thing how we could ever achieve the right thing? In fact, right deeds seem to have waned and passed into oblivion, whereas we still feel to be doing the right thing on a daily basis. You know what? A blind person cannot lead a deployed group of soldiers. It's absolutely impossible! This is because one cannot proffer what one does not possess, in life. In a nutshell, once your existence, embodying both your past and your future, is wrong, you can hardly do the right thing. Because, your existence controls your daily actions, and your daily actions are you in manifestation.

Additionally, do you know why human beings often hardly agree? This is usually as a result of having different but conflicting stories or experiences to tell, happening as a result of our diverse environments: some rural/local, some urban/western, and some international. No doubt. In this case, all we need to do is to keep doing the right thing wherever we find ourselves. There is no human being who does not know and/or have the knowledge of good and bad, making it rather enjoyably easy enough to merge with any kind of stranger, once your existence is justifiable. Sincerely speaking, the world in which we live has never for once been faulty; the wrong is in us. Why? Once you try to dominate or lord over the one who is at the same time trying to achieve the same aim against you or the other, there must be a fatal clash, yielding to several other clashes. It is clearly revealed by Jean-Paul Sartre (in *Why Write?)* that the world is lethargic, and that it is rather humans who make it lively as though it were a living thing or being. You see? Why blame the *innocent* world, then? Thus, work on your own personal world and don't think of doctoring the one that is but *natural.* Logically, however, your own world is that natural world. But the only way you can use yours (the personal or individual one) to influence the natural one is to do only that which is determined by *nature.* Work on yourself, and nature will surely reward you, because it's not humans who reward humans; it is *nature* that rewards humans. This is why if one receives any unnatural reward, one soon turns has-been. And the reward from nature neither wanes nor perishes, clearly revealed in the book of James 1:17, saying: *Every good and perfect gift is from above...* Isn't that great? For instance, any country that sees doing things truly evenly as to making it beneficial to even the obviously incapacitated or less-privileged citizens, corruption is never ever legalized, making life there always more like that happening on another planet other than the planet earth. Whereas, it is still perfectly (happening) on the same planet (earth) and in the same world. Therefore, a great deal of what goes wrong in a country or among a people is aided by the government. On the other hand, it is still individual humans who now group themselves to form a people's government. In that case, if their various, *individual worlds* are faulty, the government will certainly be faulty and pretty unfavourable to many. You see? So the only way to better the world is to work on oneself. And so do no longer say: *if I cannot beat them, I join them.* If you carelessly or insensitively allow an oiled finger to be and fail to clean it up on the spot, you soon find the others equally oiled. And so always endeavour to run away from things that are rather to mar or cause a dent on your precious existence. Instead, use yours to influence and make right whatever you discover is faulty. That is the true effectiveness of your glorious existence! But remember, your past must not be faulty, because that is your identity.

Furthermore, why it is naturally unavoidable to have to do the right things always is because that is what keeps our existence valid. For example, a diver with an expired driving licence is bound to be arrested at any time – I mean whenever he is caught – because he has run out of the validation of his right to use the motorways. Likewise, once you stop doing the right things, your existence is not only at stake in the *hand* of nature, but also already out of the validity of true and blessed living. You see? Pitiably, a great many persons, nowadays, crave for war and violence, having known the extent to which they've ruined and run out of their existence validation, now ready for the wrath of nature – you know what I mean. The highest benefit in life is the attainment of a good, unquestionable destiny!

Chapter Nine

What Can Mar One's Future?

*The security of one's future is determined by
one's past and one's subsequent deeds.*

It is indeed painful that many people desire to attain and
enjoy a good future but they often do not know how to go
about it. In fact, a good future often slips off the grips of
people when the need for it is even higher than ever. Why? It
is most often than not caused by ill foundation. If the past to
a good future is unnatural, the enjoyment of it is not certain.
Every good future needs a good past; otherwise, it is prone
to be thwarted. Why? The human past is the protective
device to the future, by providing with it the immunity with
which to live. This makes us to understand that no future
can ever be without a good past. The issue is because the
human future is naturally *fed* by its past. However, one's

current or subsequent deeds can also mar one's precious future, leading us to our main discourse. Two things are capable of destroying any precious future: a bad past and one's current negative deeds. If your past is negative, your future will be haunted, just as both your precious future and your past can easily be squashed by your latter horrible deeds. This, then, reveals that one cannot even attain a bit of a good future if one's past is negative. Worse still is insensitively using your latter unethical deeds to crush your existence – your past and your future. At this juncture, let's see what can be considered as a bad past and what usually causes it. Before we talk about that proper, first, I'd want us to be rather logical in our reflective thinking as to know, and bear in mind, that every past was once a future. Now know also that every bit of what you did while your today's past was a current future is what now constitutes both your today's past and another current future. You know that now? Good. Let's, then, talk about what can bring about a bad past. The human past evolves based on actions. We all know that actions are performed with the help of the human potential energy, which tells us that every human action is based on movement. In like manner, the human movement cannot act without having to obey the law of thought – your wish. This therefore reveals that every human move that brings about an action is but deliberate. The human mind swiftly thinks, analyzes and then concludes on a thing, before acting. Therefore, it is pretty disagreeable to hear one say that he or she never meant to perform an action, except there is something evidently wrong with his or her thinking ability. In other words, one can never live or act right if one's mind often thinks evil. And that is the secret of creating a good personality – your existence.

However, a great many individuals often find it immensely difficult to create a good image, because they don't know how to transform their evil thoughts into a good one. Although evil thoughts are inevitable (i.e. they are bound to pop up in the mind), it is but our primary obligation, as humans, to either subdue or transform them into producing a moral result. Thus, if an evil thought eventually pops up in your mind, don't ever consider it as the solution to the situation. What is evil is naturally evil and destructive. And so the only way you can transform it into something moral is by seeing it as intrinsically evil and then avoiding it. It is when this happens that a good thought can then emerge, taking the place of the evil one. Despite how angry or nervous you might be, always endeavour to be very sure your intended action is ethical. In this way, you can lead a morally acceptable lifestyle. Once your lifestyle is not questionable or reprehensible, your existence can be productive. And the productiveness of one's existence is of one's past – your prior living. Once your past is productive, your future is in a sure happy, productive state, as well. For instance, any business organization that fails to invest cannot harvest anything, just like planting. And so your future is your past in the current. On the other hand, as we prior said, regardless of how you had managed to secure a glowing past but later become insensitive and, then, deviate from the principle of proper or ethical living, your future can still be marred. No doubt. If you would not shed human blood in time past but suddenly decide to, you are simply destroying your past – the source of life to your future. In that case, what happens? What is capable of occurring is like the common situation whereby every living being dies when the respiratory organ is damaged. Thus, every good future with a destroyed past is bound to wither and die at any time. If you suddenly decide to do evil, you are unconsciously barricading the path of the supplier of life to your future – the road of your past. And so it is two things that can mar your future, as earlier unravelled.

It is quite a pity that a great many individuals usually think to have done good to the fullest that they would later feel like to switch to doing a little evil. No, that's not it! Once this occurs, you are bound to lose all your hard-earned, age-old, precious good! To be frank with you, doing good or living right is like breathing. When one stops breathing, what happens? In fact, you can't even think of to stop to breathe, unless you desire death. If this is inevitable, you can't stop to live right always. You see? And so your future requires your daily righteousness to be greatly uninterruptedly productive. A lot of people kill today and then repent tomorrow, thinking it's all about that. No. You know what? Both your positive and your negative deeds form a *bureaucratic* structure to your existence. They are so called because they are naturally there to carry out their inevitable function – and you cannot reverse it. In other words, your existence embodies whatever you do in life, which implies that you can hardly successfully renounce to have not committed anything while you really did it. This reveals that it's even one's existence that brings to light one's deed, be it negative or positive. And so confessing your barbaric acts cannot protect or justify your existence or personality; it could only spare your life from some immediate penalty. And if your existence constitutes both your past and your future, how, then, does your existence not valuable to you? This is the reason why people's good, sparkling futures always get suddenly crushed. The most pitiable set of humans are those who are yet to know that the only *path* to a good success is by living right on a daily basis, meanwhile they daily crave for success. Isn't that dramatically ironic? And so the essence of this chapter is for such consciousness to be created in us. On the other hand, many always believe that their unproductive past is as a result of some unwise, ancient deeds carried out by their forerunners. Why it apparently affects you is not because it is idiosyncratically effective on your own existence; it is because you believe it and so refuse to create something new for yourself – something that would suit the age and time and enable you to produce something of your desire in life. Once you say: *my father used to live like this...* you are simply dwelling your existence on some moribund platform (and you know what that means). Think in line with the age and time, and be successful. No actor can ever be behind the stage and be essential; he must be seen, through his performance, and be made essential by the audience.

In like manner, how legally well do you perform in your daily-life actions? Do you often relegate yourself to the back stage and still expect to be essential and successful? Or do you think it's doing evil or reckless things behind the stage that pays? No! You must be seen perform well and right before everyone, in a broad day light. Why do you think lightning is an inevitable spectacle of dramatization? It is because any dramatization done in the dark – and not seen and understood at all by the audience, is bound to be doubtfully unrealistic and then useless. In other words, the evil you do in the dark, thinking it is pretty smartly done, cannot be granted justice; and but so reprehensible. This is the reason why a lot of people have failed woefully in life. They always deem it fit exercising their acts in the secret, but unconscious of what darkness connotes. And so, in relation to the notion of this chapter, in order not to mar your precious future, always endeavour your daily deeds are ethical and visible enough for justification. Otherwise, regardless of how glowingly justifiable your past might be, your current negative deeds can mar your future overnight. And your ruined future is but your current past ruined, as well. To make it plainer, what affects your current future equally affects your past. Furthermore, a great many individuals care much too little about their past and their future because they are pretty yet to realize that they are themselves their past and their future – those constituting the essence of their being alive. This, then, reveals that one cannot be separated from one's past and one's future. That is why it is characteristic of humans to address any successful individual in lieu of his or her success, for instance. It is because they see that success of yours as you but that which is functioning in an abstract, successful medium; likewise if an individual is unsuccessful. You see? The reason is because it is naturally indisputable to every individual that the effectiveness of one's existence is what makes something of life. And so if one is not positively effective enough to make something of life, one is got to blame nobody else. And leading and maintaining a good lifestyle is the sole key to being productive in life. This then buttresses the essence of this chapter, which maintains that one's future can still be equally marred if one stops leading a good life to the end. Hmmm! Is that not a situational irony? In fact, this is partly what usually turns many to has-beens, in life. It is either their past negative deeds begin haunting them later, or they eventually set up an absolutely contrary life principle to that of nature, due to their unsteady moral attitude. In a nutshell, the good of someone must be maintained from the beginning to the end, at least to the level of its beginning to speak for one in a positive way.

Chapter Ten

What Are Usually Found in a Good Future?

The human future is but like a tree planted for the purpose of fruit yielding. Thus, a future can truly be called only when its core purpose is realized.

The purpose of the preceding insight is to act as a prompting element to our understanding of this chapter, which tells us that a future is worth it only when its complete, desirable features are embodied in it. This chapter's concern is like the practical scenario of someone who successfully secures a container from a wharf to a warehouse but is sadly unfortunate to find nothing in it, revealing that attaining a future without its features is not as important and/or ideal as securing both – the future itself and its features. Why so is because everyone's future must come, but naturally not embodying one's desired treasures. This is a major cause of a lot of people achieving but not conceiving a good future. If so, it is natural that every good future must be conceived, thereby nurturing and maintaining alongside your forthcoming future the desired features for it. Okay? This means that if you desire to achieve a new/another car, for instance, you therefore plan it in a timely manner as to achieve it in your next future. And so you simply conceive your future packages in a way of just desiring and beginning to plan towards them.

In a nutshell, the human future is like the brain of a tender human being - a child. As it is biologically and/or scientifically revealed that every tender human child is born but with an empty slate in the brain, likewise the human future; which reveals that every natural, general human future is virtually empty, requiring of the humans to fill it with their respective desired features. At the same time, everyone has the ability to fill theirs in their own way. And so, sincerely speaking, if you think letting it emerge in its natural (empty) state is what you desire, you certainly achieve it in the very way. However, this is what usually renders a lot of people unproductive in life. If you harbour any doubt, you find out soon. If this notion is considerably likeable to the empty-slate issue of a child, what is common of a child who happens not to have been properly or consciously brought up enough in the communication (speaking) aspect of child growing is what is similar to happen in the case of not realizing a good future. Are they not usually bound to speak either incoherently or not at all? And so teaching them how to communicate with conscious acts is what brings about the filling-up of their empty slates. In like manner, the human future also needs to be taught how to yield *fruits*; only that it is done in another medium. Whereas you speak for a child to respond while filling up his or her empty slate, you do both the speaking and the responding in terms of filling up your future with your desired elements. How? It is as simple as if you desire a house, you just to go get yourself engaged in some job, secure the money, and then get the house built. The process you go through before getting the house built is what amounts to filling up your future with what you desire. You understand it now? In this case, while you do the speaking, you also have to do the responding, which is exactly what has made a great many persons not to achieve what they desire, as they usually do only the *speaking* without *responding*. Again is the fact that a child could yet be struggling to respond and begin to communicate properly until he or she eventually grasps it on his or her own, while the human future requires extreme scepticism of monitoring and persistence in filling it up, until the desired result is attained. This now reveals that many usually fail simply because they are often not sceptically persistent in pursuing what they want (in life or for their future) until the desired result is achieved.

In relation to our major discourse, therefore, there are peculiar features that are usually found in a good future. A good future is indisputably worth it as it is bound to *reward/provide* you with the following packages, such as peace, joy, affluence, satisfaction, freedom, better ideas and focus, recognition and acceptance, identification, honour, influence, etc. This simple illustration made is to make us to realize how highly paramount it is for one to *fight* for the attainment of a good future. It is therefore understandable that any future maintaining a number of contents lower or less than the aforementioned is worse than not worthy of praise. And that's why it is rather in your power to fight for yourself the kind of future that you desire. Two things tend to bring forth a bad future: idleness and non-persistence. An idle person is half a foot away from the realization of a bad future, just as the latter is capable of making someone to make an ill U-turn – and you know what that means. If a farmland having nothing cultivated in it is in no way prospective of harvests, any idle person is millions of miles away from a good future. You must cultivate in your future today, to harvest your crops tomorrow. And so the achievement of a good future can never be done by only desiring; you also have to be persistent as you work towards it. Therefore, as we prior said, you are in the position to work out exactly what you expect of your future. For a better understanding, therefore, let's consider what usually becomes of someone who may have felt idling about yesterday would reward him or her today. Thus, one's today's idleness is one's tomorrow's wretchedness, implying that you get to experience the negative nature of your today's unproductive or zero effort, tomorrow. This assertion is even justifiably truer than we could imagine as it is obvious that everybody does not smile in the same fashion at a new dawn. Therefore what constitutes this natural human future is everybody being equally alive to have seen the next dawn, but certainly not having the same feelings at it. Whereas some are bound to complain or think negatively, regardless of their still being alive to experience another new dawn, lamenting for their having to face more hardship, others are bound to be even more grateful to God for granting them another brand new day that is to yield for them the accomplishment of their already-attained contracts that will make them happier and more successful people, in life. You see? This, then, unveils to us how it is pretty in our own power to strive for what we desire of life. And that's why it is immutably divine for heaven to smoothen your effort towards the attainment of your heart desires.

This implies that one does not have any one to blame to have not achieved a good future, since everyone is to strive for the type of future that they please. On the other hand, why a great many persons cannot come up with a single heart-desire is because they don't even know what they are capable of. Yes. It is true because your ability to desire a thing is pioneered by your personal reasoning capability. Having successfully reasoned and desired a thing, you then have the drive to go for it, by beginning to practise your logical thought or idea. This makes it believable that a good future is worked for, whereas the natural future is definite to come but in a fashion that is not all that desirable. If you walk down the street in a critical observance of the people you come by, you will find that it is not every one of them that is equally busy as to engaging themselves in one rational, productive thing or the other, which tells us that it is far from fortuitous for some people's futures to be bad. The purpose of this scenario is to enable us to know why it is not every one of us that is bound to achieve a good future. And so God has already given us a general future out of which we are to make what we desire. If someone gives you an acre of land and you fail to cultivate in it, in due season, you certainly have yourself to blame by the time your fellows begin to enjoy their precious harvests. This makes it ideal to follow suit when everyone is working, in order to enjoy the next future with them. Let's consider this of the man who was equally successful in making money with his friend. Afterwards, it was tactfully thought out by his friend how it might be very wise of them to have the money invested in some lucrative business, instead of lavishing it. Although it sounded considerably good an idea to this man, his narrow-mindedness kept him on a very high mountain of absurdity and disbelief against his friend's precious idea. Unfortunately, it wasn't until he had already squandered the whole money that he realized the tenacious consequence of his naivety, when his friend was already enjoying the precious yields of his investment. This also reveals that not until you already have a mental picture of how your tomorrow (future) should be will you ever have the appropriate zest or focus to work towards it. Also is when you ought to begin working towards what you want, as many do not know the appropriate time to work towards their future.

Furthermore, for us to be able to work towards our future appropriately, it is needful to know the various types of future that we have, which are here logically segmented as the **current future**, the **immediate future**, and the **far future**. As it was revealed much earlier that we logically do not have a *present* but a *current future*, let's talk about the above future types one after the other. The current future is the faithful account of one's past. In other words, it is the overall account of both your *past current future* and your *past immediate future*. And so one's current future should be highly worth it, based on one's conscious effort. One's immediate future is that which operates as its name implies. The immediate future is that which gives a faithful but quick account of one's actions. It brings the immediate future result of one's just-carried-out actions. For example, one is liable to do something wrong and get caught immediately and be penalized soon afterwards. In like manner, based on one's actions, one who was broke in the morning could become financially buoyant before evening that same day. These are the elements of the immediate future. The far future, as the name implies, is that which gives the overall account of both your current future and your immediate future. This could be based on some long-term investment or budgets, some seriously elongated planning, or the adjustment of strategies. Based on any of the above, the actualization of one's future is bound to be delayed, but it is usually complete in its sense. The far future is that which usually brings about one's next overall future, thereby becoming another current future. It happens also in the same fashion with the human past. In a nutshell, having known the various types of the human future, one may now know the very type of future that one looks forward to attaining. It is also in order that one may know why the human future differs; likewise the human past.

Chapter Eleven

The Glory for the Attainment of a Good Past

A crown or reward is usually given but only to the one who merits it.

As clearly as we all know, every glorification is inextricably tied to a reward, be it done verbally or tangibly, which makes it pretty mandatory to strive for a reward. Before one gets crowned as king, for instance, one happens to have worked very convincingly enough, either legally or illegally. In other words, a political aspirant is bound to be granted his or her aspiration on account of his or her convincing political records/reports, skills or capabilities. But in the aspect of the human past, nobody gets glorified by a bad future, determining the kind of reward one gets to receive. Whereas every good past has something positive to offer, no bad past has anything positive to offer. This is because good deeds are bound to coalesce and form something meaningfully rewarding or productive, whereas bad ones instead heap unnecessarily and eventually collapse, bringing about one's detestable merit. This is the reason why it is not only rewarding to attain a good past, but also ideal as it is bound to glorify one. If one's past is good, one is liable to achieve so many good things. Whereas a good past brings about a good record, a bad one does otherwise. And, sincerely speaking, the effective nature of one's kind of past extends not only to one's existence, but also that of one's descendants. It's like a legacy. It is here germane we get ourselves strongly acquainted with what another one of my books reveals, entitled: *The Power of a Good Legacy*, which is highly virtual in expatiating the issue of *legacy*. At this juncture, we may have to leave the word *past*, and face the word *record*. Whereas the one is apparently controversial, the other is pretty near-to-door, which is bound to enhance our understanding of this chapter. The issue is that it is absolutely impossible for one to renounce one's *record*, whereas people can tactfully disclaim their ugly pasts as traceable to their progenitors. However, whether or not you see yourself culpable for your past, the effectiveness of it lies on your existence, be it positive or negative. And that's why I would we see it as rather a record, so that one could easily admit it. Because admitting a thing gives you a chance to make it as you please. Although your past is more or less the collection of your various life records, still conceive it like a record. This is what will help you to feel better responsible for your past.

In essence, your past requires your full responsibility to make it right. It means that if you are half responsible in nurturing it, it is bound to stray off your desired direction for it, creating for you something purely less than what can reward and/or honour one in life. You see? So your extreme responsibility is required here. A good past rewards or provides you with all that you want to enjoy your current future (you wouldn't see it as a *present,* as you are liable to relax). And so be aware that what you do now is what turns your past for better, which later rewards you. But at the same time, let's consider the following words: *rewarding* and *providing.* Whereas the one is based not on consciousness, the other purely is. If you live a natural life that you do not desire anything for yourself, your past equally rewards you based on your natural living, whether or not the reward is positive. On the other hand, your past is bound to provide you with what you want on account of your heart-desire. In other words, no desiring, no providing (you with anything), just as there is sure rewarding for natural living. Overall, let's be reminded that one's new/latest past is as equally embodied in the current future (literally known as present) as one's next future. But the human latest past is ever barely conceived as something new because there is no clear-cut boundary between it and the far one, and so they are believed to be interwoven at all times; likewise the human future which is as much barely separable from the past. And so an all-round job must be done, to attain a good past that is bound to glorify you.

Furthermore, if your predecessors died with some horrible past that could not glorify them in any way, that past of theirs died with their own past existence; nothing affects you from theirs. This is like in the case of a bad father and a good son. Although the man could be that bad, his son is bound to be honoured in life; because they are entirely different existences. And so if one is not honoured, one is not doing well in life. The glory of your good past gets to everyone that relates to/with you. It could either be in the way of your helping them in one way or the other, or the people (out there) speaking rather glowingly of them on account of your appealing lifestyle. Conversely, your behaviour could be that horrible, but certainly not as much as affecting other existences related to you; because you are yourself a different existence. Anyways, no matter how bad you could be, don't be as much as beginning to destroy other people's things; because yours are equally destructible. It is in this way the effectiveness of an existence can cause some cross-existential destruction. This is why it is often a general thing of joy when one successfully attains a good past. If you do something ordinarily good, you get glorified accordingly. But if you do something extraordinarily good, the glory of your reward is bound to extend to those around you, let alone when you do something good that is generationally or globally felt. This makes doing good differ, in general. And that's why your past is bound to reward and glory you based on your overall effort. Therefore if you want the glory of your past to be enjoyable not only to you but also to those around you, you now have to create such consciousness towards the kind of what you do on a daily basis. And also be reminded that your daily acts are your past – that which is bound to create either something glorious or inglorious.

Chapter Twelve

Does Every Human Existence Deserve a Good Past?

Is there any sane human being that abhors greatness? If none, is the answer to this chapter not obvious? Anyway, we find out soon.

If the human past is doubtless the *forerunner* of the future, and it is also everything found in our future, it is therefore succinct that we each deserve but a good one, as none can ever be great without a good past in one's future. This is pretty indisputable as it is similar to the fact that no woman ever gets pregnant of a child and gets delivered of it immediately. No! Every woman is bound to be pregnant of a baby for, basically, nine months before her delivery of the baby can naturally occur. You see? This confirms that one's future can never be created and simultaneously enjoyed. But unfortunately, this is where a great many people often get it all wrong; by always conceiving the good of their future as to manifest right at the time of the creation of it. M—m! The reason is because they haven't known that the current future – that which later coalesces with the past – is that which is used to create the good that is usually embodied in another future. And that's why you are bound to be creating the various levels of abundance that you desire for your futures to come. And so this principle is clearly inevitable. In relation to the very concern of this chapter, therefore, everyone deserves a good past, in order to earn a meaningful living. Conversely, many often desire to attain a good future, instead of a good past. Well, although desiring a good future is no wrong, it is germane to know when that desire is bound to be realized. The reason is because if you are not aware of when exactly that your next-future desire is bound to come, you will have caused yourself a great deal of wretchedness and absurdity before you finally achieve it.

In a nutshell, if you desire your subsequent future to be good, you work it out now; because this is the accurate time. But if you desire your next future to be good and you feel you are to work it out when it has already come, just be aware to realize your aim in the one after it. You get it now? Yes, it cannot be done otherwise! At this juncture, we can pontificate that many have failed because of not having this simple notion. You know what? I can surmise that a lot of people, who are unproductive today, always feel less concerned with their current meaningless standard of living because of the hope of what they feel they have already desired for their next future, but obviously unaware of the time of the actualization of that desire of theirs. And so what are we saying? This is why it is the sole concern of the concept of this chapter, by revealing to us all that it takes to achieve a good past, making this chapter to hold in high esteem the notion that the good of the human past is what makes the human future. And this portrays that for a future not to be realized in absurdity of thought, wretchedness of living, or stagnation of existence, the human past is got to take its divine course. It asserts that anything one experiences today, is what was created by one yesterday. No doubt. And so if a future well functioning is a past well created, everyone deserves a good past. So, one's past is one's hope. Therefore, no good past; no good future, irreversibly leading to the attainment of a horrible, deserted existence. Furthermore, no responsible man and woman ever plunge into marriage without first idealizing knowing each other's background (due to some significant reasons had about marriage). This is because the past is naturally believed to be the controller or holder of the existence of every human being. And that's why no one can successfully renounce his past deeds, at least not before *nature* itself. Why, then, can't we strive for the attainment of a good past? I could remember very vividly when my dad was planning to build a new house. His desire was never achieved at the time of his speaking; it was after a considerable period, which resulted from his having to have been saving little by little from his monthly earnings with extraordinary consciousness. You see? It depicts that the good of your future is achieved from/pioneered by your yesterday's overall effort. Furthermore, your today's effort is the determiner of how your next future will be. If you play pranks with your boss today, you are bound to be fired tomorrow, after he must have recounted all your preceding illegal deeds. You see? This unveils that your bad future is the reward of your detestable past. And so live right today, to earn well tomorrow. And one thing I like pretty much about the past is that it does not only reward one, but also glorify one, as it's lucidly revealed in the preceding chapter. And since it is only a good past that glorifies one, it should be understood as everyone's *game*!

Chapter Thirteen

A Good Past as a Success Ladder for One's Descendants

The smooth existence of parents is the guarantee for the success of their seeds.

Every child born is bound to have their existing parents, whether or not they are legally together. And their parentage is the instrument that begins to nurture the existence of that child at that early age. This is bound to happen as a child at this early age obviously does not have the consciousness of human existence. A child at this early age only knows how to sleep after bathing and eating, wake up when he or she pleases, and then crave for some food more. You see? It implies that a child at a tender age naturally does not think logically for any reason. In other words, he or she lives purely at the expense of their parents. And so the duty of the parents is dual and remains until their children are grown up enough to begin to think/reason logically for themselves, making their age of emancipation the determiner. Even as that, the parents still have a great deal of work to do in directing their children on moral existence, by getting them fully acquainted with all the necessary moral tips that they require. And so the parents obviously have more than a lot to do for their children, in order that they may have a smooth and/or meaningful existence. This philosophy is highly critical as it requires the parents to have to use the enormously meaningful functionality of their own existence to create and direct that of their children, until they are grown up enough to understand what their parents have been doing for them all through their childhood years. This is very important as to the fact that, at this early age, the children's security, shelter and sociological endeavours are to be pioneered and regulated by their parents' existence.

In a nutshell, since a child is yet to have an effective existence enough to enable him or her to do without his or her parents' own, that of the parents is what works for the whole family. This assertion stands indisputable as it is realistic that a child having a reputable family background is bound to live freely or in a violence-free manner in all his or her endeavours. But there is this *instrument* that guarantees this diverse immunity for the whole family at this stage – a good past. This instrument functions in diverse ways, as it is capable of making training your children instead communal, in the sense that it urges one's community members to help protect, advice and separate one's children from any form of danger, in the absence of their parents. It also helps luck them into their individual pursuits, as they are bound to be spoken pretty glowingly of wherever they find themselves. You see? This now requires one's past to be exceedingly good, as every good past is to speak but not necessarily beyond the overall degree of its goodness. In other words, if one's past is not as good and effective enough as to spread to the benefit of one's children, one cannot overstretch it. Furthermore, a lot of children, nowadays, suffer rather innocently because of the kind of existence that is traceable to them from their parents. Most often than not, you find that the overall degree of the goodness of the past of most parents is so limited or minute that even the parents themselves can barely enjoy it. In a case of such, what is liable of becoming their children? In fact, they are bound not to find the parentage of their parents funny at all; because of their having to acquaint themselves rather too early with the strife for a meaningful and fun living. You see? Therefore attaining a good past is not only ideal for you, but also for your descents. Even worse is when one had done something downright wrong before having children; one's children normally become more or less a scapegoat to that deed, as most illegal deeds are bound not to act rather fast. To confirm this, let's consider what the book of 1 Kings 21:29 says: *See how Ahab has humbled himself before Me, I will not bring the calamity in his days; in the days of his son I will bring the calamity on his house.* You see? This reveals that most parents' transgressions are so indelible that it is their children who are bound to suffer from them, making human existence considerably scientific in nature. And so your descendants are bound to enjoy not only your glorious inheritance, but also your good name, once your past is positively effective enough. It is even greater than all the material things you deem necessary to keep in stock for them. Therefore the focus of this chapter is nothing else than to unveil to us the diverse functionality of a good past and why it is everyone's *meat* to bite.

As you see the bone of contention of this chapter, which sees a good past as a *success ladder* for one's descents, it is vivid that the smooth success of any child is considerably tied to the extraordinarily productive existence of his or her parents. However, this assertion is not in any way to mean that a child cannot grow on his or her own and still be successful. No! It naturally unveils that a child's successfulness tends to be delayed and sort of struggled for when their parents' overall success degree is not effective enough to facilitate theirs. Understood? Good. Thus, a child is bound to think big as does his father; likewise if his father's logical reasoning is limited. And so what affects a child's parents logically, equally affects that child. But mind you, what we are talking about is a child who is yet reasoning logically on his or her own. However, the grown-ups also get pretty affected when they find themselves in communal or societal activities; as the people might be tempted to trace and eventually analyze their parents' past-to-current life, for one reason or the other. And so the actualization of a good past should be made a priority by every human existence. More explicitly the concern of this chapter, therefore, the corporate existence of a child's parents is what stands as the past that keeps him or her going, until he or she has the ability to create a different one for him or herself. And so that's why a child is equally liable to suffer the peril of his or her parents' punishable deeds. In essence, your descendants require your glorious existence, to earn a smooth living and success!

Chapter Fourteen

The Past as an Oasis for the Future

Any nation without a treasury enough (to sustain her inhabitants) is bound to crumble and eventually be made an appendage to another nation.

Before we begin the discussion of this chapter, let's take an intelligent look at the dictionary meaning of the word *oasis*. In other words, what is *oasis*? The following are its two different meanings held in high esteem by the English Encarta Dictionaries:

1. **Fertile land in desert:** fertile ground in a desert where the level of underground water rises to or near ground level, and where plants grow and travellers can replenish water supplies.

2. **Place or time of relief:** a place or period that gives relief from a troubling or chaotic situation.

Having considered and digested the foregoing, it is obvious that we now know what *oasis* means and its indefeasible nature. As lucidly as it is evident since my childhood years till date, it is indisputable that everyone deserves an individual oasis, to survive. However, oasis differs from one individual to another. Oasis can be in the form of a purse, bag or briefcase, or something strongly strategized. In fact, in this modern world, both men and women now make do with the pockets of their wear, coupled with their ages-old uses of portfolios (for men) and purses (for women). This art remains inevitable, as no one can live otherwise without encountering socialization difficulties. And why nobody can successfully do without it is because it implies trying to work against nature. Ok just imagine someone not having at least a sum of 500 Naira secured/saved anywhere for his sustenance! Do you know what that means? It means making oneself unavoidably living at the mercy of the person who has an oasis somewhere. You see? And so the essence of this chapter is but to let us know what it means to have an oasis.

Furthermore, to make this discourse rather near-to-door enough for everyone's profitable understanding, let's consider what people usually do when they go out shopping. One definitely leaves home with separated amounts of money for various assignments: the first for the going trip, the second for the purchasing proper, and the third for the return trip. What you do is to first keep your second and your third amounts in your mobile oasis – particularly your purse, bag or pocket. Once you don't abide by this principle, you certainly scramble your purchase plan. This now hands us over to the main concern of this chapter, which unravels the fact that the past is the oasis of the future. This, then, reveals that every human past should be made and filled up with everything necessary for one's future not to be lacking of anything. And so for a past to be an oasis for its future, it must be worked on based on the following principles:

The Natural Principle: this maintains the philosophy that the human past does not only possess the ability to create and to nurture the various human futures, but also to guide and to smoothen their affairs.

The Mother Principle: this upholds the notion that the human past is but a *mother of many children*; thereby working assiduously to ensuring that her children - the next/current future, the immediate future, and the far future - lack but nothing necessary.

The Example Principle: this maintains the consciousness that the human past is the pathfinder for all the different segments of the human future; thereby working based on the law of morality and justice, in order that the others would work in the same fashion.

The Posterity Principle: this is the most sensitive and effective principle. It is the one that questions the excesses of the human past, regulates its deeds, etc., in order to make the past a true pathfinder for (and not a hindrance to) the next generations to come.

In a nutshell, any human past that is not created based on the foregoing principles cannot be a true oasis for the future. Thus, it must be based on each and every one of the foregoing principles, for one's future not to exist in nothingness. By the concept of this chapter, we mean to unravel the fact that the human past is that which possesses all that it takes for the human future to exist in abundance. And so for the past to have this possessive and productive ability, it must be worked on as such. Explicitly, therefore, everything possessed by one's past is as a result of the overall effort of the individual involved, implying that any past that is not productive enough to make one's future appreciably sustaining and enjoyable is pioneered by one's idleness level.

Thus, no past naturally possesses the necessary requirements to qualify it as an oasis for the future; they are to be filled by the individual involved. And that's why a great many individuals instead lament at the emptiness of their futures, today. The reason is because they failed to fill their pasts yesterday, for today, with those necessary requirements. You see? There's no how the future can in any way be in plenty without having filled the past with all the necessary elements, yesterday. Furthermore, living right daily with an evergreen consciousness of the fact that your current deeds are what produce your future expectations is the only guarantee that one's future can be in abundance. In this way, your past would have automatically possessed the certificate for living in abundance for your future, before your future would emerge. Therefore, in order to secure a future in abundance, don't give up on your today's effort. Strive enormously, to grab abundantly. *Your past is your future oasis!*

Chapter Fifteen

The Well-Merged Past and Future: Living Without Fear!

Although a man and a woman can forcefully be married with each other, they are bound to lose bond and eventually sag apart like a virgin tarred road suddenly quaked and splashed apart rather greedily by some wandering caterpillar. So also are the human past and the future; they cannot be wrongly merged in a forceful manner with each other.

A bridge is worse than anything known to be obviously fragile once the merging of its segments is ill or incautiously done. Once this happens, the regret of it usually springs so high, as it can hardly ever be restored without repeating the whole process. Similarly is what usually occurs whenever the roof of a shoe is but not properly merged with its sole. When it pulls off in an untimely manner, it demonstrates the fact that either a little attention was given to the making of it or the material used particularly for the merging was but a substandard one. This, then, unveils how highly cautiously sensitive one should be when it comes to merging one thing with another. Thus, a little attention should not be given to it; one has to be extremely conscious of the whole process. However, very hardly seen nowadays is one who really understands and can act based on the exact principle of merging. To a large extent, this has caused more harm than good to a great many persons out there, which now leads us into the smooth, well-lit, intellectual arena of the crowning concept of this chapter.

As rightly illustrated at the preamble of this chapter, the concept of this chapter is overwhelmingly likeable to that of bridge making, as they possess similar characteristics. When we say the past and the future, there are lucidly two different concepts involved. Also is when we look forward to making a bridge; two opposing and/or separated sides are in question. And since they are not in agreement with each other, something downright technical has to be done to get them agreeable to each other. In the case of the bridge, a mental picture of how it's usually linked from one opposing side to the other, making them agree, is worth creating to get this scenario rather explicable enough. Although in the case of the past and the future there are equally two different things involved, unlike the visible nature of the bridge, that which links up the human past and the future is purely abstract, making it pretty more technical to be approached and processed right. You see? This unfortunately happens to be the most neglected of all! Why? Well, it is most likely traceable to the inability to approach it all.

This is, however, the essence of this chapter; unravelling how even much easier it is to approach the merging of your past and your future right. If you carry out a critical analysis on the boundary existing between the past and the future, you will discover that it is although counter-intuitive but very tender the blend into the two. In other words, their boundary cannot be addressed in isolation. This is the reason why one ever hardly talks about the past without relating it to the future, or the future without the past. They are inextricably interwoven. In a nutshell, what can one do to attain a well-merged past and future? Since the boundary between the past and the future is not as visibly and easily correctible as a bridge, one has to be extremely consistent in one's daily living. In other words, one ought to work rather consistently towards what one expects in one's future, today, until one's expectation is finally achieved. Once there exists a loophole, you possibly lose everything. And so if you are living right daily, you've got to try and do it to the end. The reason is because, like the bridge, no boundary can be so called if it does not have full contacts with both segments. Do you now see why a great many usually fail in life? For instance, one looks forward to becoming a medical doctor without carrying out consistent studies – how can that be? You behave well now; you behave ill the next seconds – are you sure you are not breaking or disintegrating that boundary? That is the question! Therefore, to maintain that boundary to the end, *consistency* is the sole *tool* to use. If you wish to enjoy your tomorrow, endure the use of this tool today.

Furthermore, why this is so important is because of how pitiable it is for someone to use his own hands to destroy his existence, by allowing that boundary to break down – just like what is usually experienced of a collapsed bridge. And remember, successfully linking up your past with your future, in an illegal fashion, does not still guarantee your success; because nature soon finds you out (and you know that means). When this happens, it is usually worse than to have not attempted a thing of such at all. This is unfortunately the means that has mostly destroyed so many lives, today. But once you try and lead a simple, moral life daily, you get your past and your future successfully merged with each other without running a single headache! To successfully do this, the following has to be applied on a daily basis: selflessness, cheerfulness, conscientiousness, contentedness, humaneness, oneness, and, above all, a consistency of living. In this way, your past and your future are successfully well-merged! When this happens, you know what? *You then live not only successfully, but also without fear*! Happy successful living and existence!